Math in Focus®
Singapore Math
by Marshall Cavendish

Activity Book

Author

Melvin Teo

 **Marshall Cavendish**
Education

U.S. Distributor

Houghton
Mifflin
Harcourt

COMMON CORE

© 2013 Marshall Cavendish International (Singapore) Private Limited

Published by Marshall Cavendish Education
An imprint of Marshall Cavendish International (Singapore) Private Limited
Times Centre, 1 New Industrial Road, Singapore 536196
Customer Service Hotline: (65) 6213 9444
E-mail: tmesales@sg.marshallcavendish.com
Website: www.marshallcavendish.com/education

Distributed by
Houghton Mifflin Harcourt
222 Berkeley Street
Boston, MA 02116
Tel: 617-351-5000
Website: www.hmheducation.com/mathinfocus

Cover: ©Tim Laman/Getty Images

First published 2013

Math in Focus® Activity Book Course 2
ISBN 978-0-547-57905-4

Printed in Singapore

4 5 6 7 8   1401   17 16 15 14 13
4500455968   B C D E

Contents

CHAPTER 1

The Real Number System

Lesson 1.3 Activity   Irrational Numbers **1**

Project   Who is Rational? **5**

CHAPTER 2

Rational Number Operations

Lesson 2.1 Activity   Adding Integers in a Magic Square **9**

Project   Operation Integer **15**

CHAPTER 3

Algebraic Expressions

Lesson 3.4 Activity   Expanding Algebraic Expressions **19**

Lesson 3.6 Activity   Writing Algebraic Expressions **25**

Project   Factoring Algebraic Expressions **29**

CHAPTER 4

Algebraic Equations and Inequalities

Lesson 4.1 Activity   Matching Equivalent Expressions **35**

Lesson 4.2 Activity   Algebraic Expressions and Equations **41**

Project   Solving Algebraic Inequalities **45**

CHAPTER 5

Direct and Inverse Proportion

Lesson 5.1 Activity   Direct Proportion **49**

Project   Decorating Boards **55**

CHAPTER 6

Angle Properties and Straight Lines

Lesson 6.1 Activity   Identifying Complementary and
Supplementary Angles **61**

Lessons 6.2–6.3 Activity   Identifying Congruent Angles **65**

Project   Interior and Exterior Angles **71**

CHAPTER 7

Geometric Construction

Lessons 7.1–7.3 Activity   Inscribed and Circumscribed
Circles of a Triangle **75**

Project   Cyclic Quadrilateral **79**

CHAPTER 8

Volume and Surface Area of Solids

Lessons 8.2–8.4 Activity   Finding the Maximum Volume **83**

Project   Finding the Minimum Surface Area **91**

CHAPTER 9

Statistics

Lesson 9.4 Activity   Random Sampling **95**

Lesson 9.5 Activity   Making a Prediction **99**

Project   Letter Frequency **103**

CHAPTER 10

Probability

Lesson 10.3 Activity   Comparing Experimental and
Theoretical Probability **107**

Project   Probability Modeling **111**

Solutions **121**

Introducing Math in Focus® Activity Book

The *Activity Book*, created to complement **Math in Focus®: Singapore Math by Marshall Cavendish**, provides additional projects and activities to deepen students' mathematical experiences. These projects and activities allow students to model mathematics, reason abstractly about new content, make sense of non-routine problems, and persevere in solving them.

Using the Activity Book

The *Activity Book* contains either a paper-and-pencil activity or a technology activity to accompany one lesson in each chapter of *Math in Focus®*. It also contains a project for each chapter that can be done either with a partner or a small group. Some activities and projects can be used as an alternate approach to what is taught in the Student Book, and others are extensions of what is in the Student Book. Each activity and project includes a scoring rubric, recording sheets and templates for students, and an answer key with solutions.

The *Activity Book* is also available online and on the Teacher One Stop.

BLANK

The Real Number System

Lesson 1.3 Activity: Irrational Numbers

Teacher's Guide

Type of activity	Hands-on activity
Objective	Reinforce understanding of irrational numbers.
Materials	• Ruler • Protractor • Scissors • Glue
Time	15–20 min
Ability levels	Mixed
Prerequisite skill	Construct a square using a ruler and a protractor.
Grouping	Students should work in pairs.
Assessment of students' learning	See Lesson 1.3 Activity: Rubric.

Lesson 1.3 Activity
Rubric

Category	4	3	2	1
Mathematical concepts	Explanation shows complete understanding of the mathematical concepts used to solve the problem(s).	Explanation shows substantial understanding of the mathematical concepts used to solve the problem(s).	Explanation shows some understanding of the mathematical concepts needed to solve the problem(s).	Explanation shows very limited understanding of the underlying concepts needed to solve the problem(s) OR is not written.
Reflection	The reflection shows clear thought and effort. The learning experience being reflected upon is relevant and meaningful to student and learning goals.	The reflection shows a lot of thought and effort. Student makes attempts to demonstrate relevance, but the relevance is unclear in reference to learning goals.	The reflection shows some thought and effort. Some sections of the reflection are irrelevant to student and/or learning goals.	The reflection is superficial. Most of the reflection is irrelevant to student and/or learning goals.

Lesson 1.3 Activity
Irrational Numbers

Step 1   Use a ruler and protractor to draw squares with sides 2 inches and 1 inch, respectively.

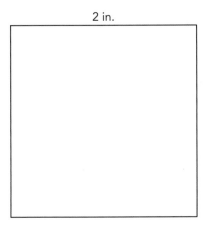

2 in.

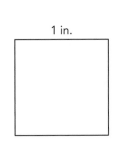

1 in.

Step 2   Cut out the squares.

Step 3   Fold the larger square in half and cut it into two congruent rectangles.

Step 4   Draw a diagonal in each rectangle. Cut along each diagonal to create four congruent right triangles.

Step 5   Arrange the four right triangles around the sides of the smaller square so that a larger square is formed with the smaller square in its center.

Step 6   Glue the square that you made on a piece of paper.

Step 7   Answer the questions on the Student Recording Sheet.

Lesson 1.3 Activity
Student Recording Sheet

1. Find the total area of the new square.

2. Based on your answer to Question 1, find the length of one side of the new square.

3. Using the ruler, find the approximate length of one side of the new square to the nearest tenth of an inch.

4. Compare your answers to Questions 2 and 3.

   a) What can you conclude from the answers?

   b) Draw a number line and graph the length of the side of the new square on it.

Reflection

5. Describe what you learned about irrational numbers from this activity.

CHAPTER 1   The Real Number System

Project: Who is Rational?

Teacher's Guide

Common Core	
Common Core State Standard	8.NS.1 Understand informally that every number has a decimal expansion; the rational numbers are those with decimal expansions that terminate in 0s or eventually repeat. Know that other numbers are called irrational.
Objective	Identify rational and irrational numbers using exponents.
Material	Calculator
Time	20–30 min
Ability levels	Mixed
Prerequisite skills	Identify prime numbers. Write a whole number as the product of its prime factors. Write numbers using exponents.
Grouping	Students should work in pairs.
Assessment of students' learning	See Chapter 1 Project: Rubric.

Chapter 1 Project Rubric

Category	4	3	2	1
Mathematical concepts	Explanation shows complete understanding of the mathematical concepts used to solve the problem(s).	Explanation shows substantial understanding of the mathematical concepts used to solve the problem(s).	Explanation shows some understanding of the mathematical concepts needed to solve the problem(s).	Explanation shows very limited understanding of the underlying concepts needed to solve the problem(s) OR is not written.
Mathematical reasoning	Uses complex and refined mathematical reasoning.	Uses effective mathematical reasoning.	Shows some evidence of mathematical reasoning.	Shows little evidence of mathematical reasoning.
Strategy/ Procedures	Uses an efficient and effective strategy to solve the problem(s).	Uses an effective strategy to solve the problem(s).	Uses an effective strategy to solve the problem(s) but does not do it consistently.	Does not use a effective strategy to solve the problem(s).
Working with others	Student was an engaged partner, listening to suggestions of others and working cooperatively throughout the lesson.	Student was an engaged partner but had trouble listening to others and/or working cooperatively.	Student cooperated with others, but needed prompting to stay on task.	Student did not work effectively with others.

Chapter 1 Project
Who is Rational?

Complete the table on the Student Recording Sheet:
Choose 10 whole numbers between 2 and 50. Write each number as the product of its prime factors.
Then write the number using exponents, as shown in the examples below.

Number	Prime factors	Exponent(s): even or odd?	Square root of the number
16	$2 \cdot 2 \cdot 2 \cdot 2 = 2^4$	Even	4
15	$3^1 \cdot 5^1$	Odd	3.872 ...
20	$2 \cdot 2 \cdot 5 = 2^2 \cdot 5^1$	One even, one odd	4.471 ...

Use your results to answer the questions on the Student Recording Sheet.

Chapter 1 Project
Student Recording Sheet

Number	Prime factors	Exponent(s): even or odd?	Square root of the number

1. Which of the square roots in the last column are rational numbers, and which are irrational numbers?

2. What conclusion can you draw from your results?

Rational Number Operations

Lesson 2.1 Activity: Adding Integers in a Magic Square

Teacher's Guide

Type of activity	Hands-on activity
Objective	Practise operations with integers.
Materials	• Scissors • Number cards on page 13 • Square grid on page 14
Time	20–30 min
Ability levels	Mixed
Prerequisite skills	Adding and dividing integers.
Grouping	Students should work in pairs.
Assessment of students' learning	See Lesson 2.1 Activity: Rubric.

Lesson 2.1 Activity
Rubric

Category	4	3	2	1
Mathematical concepts	Explanation shows complete understanding of the mathematical concepts used to solve the problem(s).	Explanation shows substantial understanding of the mathematical concepts used to solve the problem(s).	Explanation shows some understanding of the mathematical concepts needed to solve the problem(s).	Explanation shows very limited understanding of the underlying concepts needed to solve the problem(s) OR is not written.
Mathematical reasoning	Uses complex and refined mathematical reasoning.	Uses effective mathematical reasoning.	Shows some evidence of mathematical reasoning.	Shows little evidence of mathematical reasoning.
Working with others	Student was an engaged partner, listening to suggestions of others and working cooperatively throughout the lesson.	Student was an engaged partner but had trouble listening to others and/or working cooperatively.	Student cooperated with others, but needed prompting to stay on task.	Student did not work effectively with others.

Lesson 2.1 Activity
Adding Integers in a Magic Square

Step 1 Cut out the number cards on page 13.

Step 2 If the numbers from 1 to 9 are arranged in a square so that each row, column, and diagonal of the square adds up to 15, the numbers form a *magic square*. Experiment with different ways to get a sum of 15 using three of the number cards.

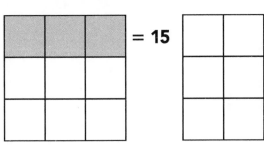 = 15

= 15

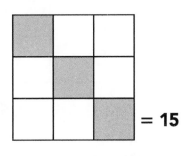 = 15

Step 3 Using the number cards, arrange the numbers in a magic square on the square grid. Then write your answer on the Student Recording Sheet.

Lesson 2.1 Activity
Student Recording Sheet

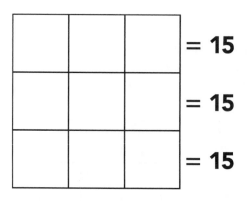

= 15 = 15 = 15 = 15

Answer these questions based on your magic square.

1. What is the sum of all nine digits used?

2. What is the relationship between the sum of the digits used and the sum of one row, column, or diagonal?

3. Subtract 5 from each number in your magic square and write the results below.

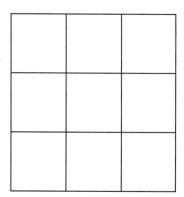

4. Is the new square also a magic square? If so, what is the sum of each row, column, or diagonal in the new square? What is the sum of all nine digits used in the new square?

Lesson 2.1 Activity
Materials

1	2	3
4	5	6
7	8	9

Lesson 2.1 Activity continued
Materials

			= 15
			= 15
			= 15

= 15 = 15 = 15 = 15

CHAPTER 2   Rational Number Operations

Project: Operation Integer

Teacher's Guide

Common Core	
Common Core State Standard	7.EE.1 Apply properties of operations as strategies to add, subtract, factor, and expand linear expressions with rational coefficients.
Objective	Reinforce understanding of operations with integers.
Materials	• Pencil • Paper
Time	30 min
Ability levels	Mixed
Prerequisite skills	Add, subtract, multiply, and divide integers.
Grouping	Students should work in groups of three.
Assessment of students' learning	See Chapter 2 Project: Rubric.

Chapter 2 Project
Rubric

Category	4	3	2	1
Mathematical concepts	Explanation shows complete understanding of the mathematical concepts used to solve the problem(s).	Explanation shows substantial understanding of the mathematical concepts used to solve the problem(s).	Explanation shows some understanding of the mathematical concepts needed to solve the problem(s).	Explanation shows very limited understanding of the underlying concepts needed to solve the problem(s) OR is not written.
Mathematical reasoning	Uses complex and refined mathematical reasoning.	Uses effective mathematical reasoning.	Shows some evidence of mathematical reasoning.	Shows little evidence of mathematical reasoning.
Working with others	Student was an engaged partner, listening to suggestions of others and working cooperatively throughout the lesson.	Student was an engaged partner but had trouble listening to others and/or working cooperatively.	Student cooperated with others, but needed prompting to stay on task.	Student did not work effectively with others.

Name: _____   Date: _____

Chapter 2 Project
Operation Integer

In this project, you will use the integers and operations below to create and simplify six expressions, using the requirements given in the table below.

Step 1 Copy and complete the following table.

Level	Mathematical expression	Answer
1a: 2 one-digit integers and 1 operator	A ____ B	
1b: 2 one- or two-digit integers and 1 operator	AB ____ CD	
2a: 3 one-digit integers and 2 operators	A ____ B ____ C	
2b: 3 one-digit integers and 2 operators with parenthesis	(A ____ B) ____ C	
2c: 3 one-digit integers and 2 operators with parenthesis	A ____ (B ____ C)	
3: 4 one-digit integers and 3 operators	A ____ B ____ C ____ D	

Replace A, B, C, and D with any of the following integers:

0   1   2   3   4   5   6   7   8   9
−1   −2   −3   −4   −5   −6   −7   −8   −9

Fill in the blanks with any of the following operations:

+   −   ×   ÷

Make sure you use a mix of positive and negative integers, and that you use each of the four operations at least once.

For example:

Level	Mathematical expression	Answer
1a	−6 + 5	−1

Step 2 Choose three of your expressions and write them in the table on the Student Recording Sheet. Then create three word problems using the three expressions. Write them on the Student Recording Sheet.

Step 3 Exchange word problems with another group and solve their word problems. Return your solutions to the other group for checking.

Chapter 2 Project
Student Recording Sheet

Level	Mathematical expression	Answer

Word problem 1:

Word problem 2:

Word problem 3:

Algebraic Expressions

Lesson 3.4 Activity: Expanding Algebraic Expressions

Teacher's Guide

Type of activity	Hands-on activity Foundational activity for students needing extra help
Objective	Reinforce the skill of expanding algebraic expressions involving decimals.
Materials	• Sets of rectangles on pages 23 and 24: – Use Set A (15 rectangles) to represent the variable term in the parentheses. – Use Set B (15 rectangles) to represent the constant term in the parentheses. • Scissors
Time	20–30 min
Ability levels	Mixed
Prerequisite skills	Multiply decimals and whole numbers. Write algebraic expressions.
Grouping	Students should work in pairs.
Assessment of students' learning	See Lesson 3.4 Activity: Rubric.

Lesson 3.4 Activity
Rubric

Category	4	3	2	1
Mathematical concepts	Explanation shows complete understanding of the mathematical concepts used to solve the problem(s).	Explanation shows substantial understanding of the mathematical concepts used to solve the problem(s).	Explanation shows some understanding of the mathematical concepts needed to solve the problem(s).	Explanation shows very limited understanding of the underlying concepts needed to solve the problem(s) OR is not written.
Reflection	The reflection shows clear thought and effort. The learning experience being reflected upon is relevant and meaningful to student and learning goals.	The reflection shows a lot of thought and effort. Student makes attempts to demonstrate relevance, but the relevance is unclear in reference to learning goals.	The reflection shows some thought and effort. Some sections of the reflection are irrelevant to student and/or learning goals.	The reflection is superficial. Most of the reflection is irrelevant to student and/or learning goals.

Name: _____   Date: _____

Lesson 3.4 Activity
Expanding Algebraic Expressions

In this activity, you will model the distributive property using areas of rectangles.

Step 1 Write an algebraic expression in this form:

$$\boxed{1}\ (\ \boxed{2}\ +\ \boxed{3}\ )$$

In the first box, write a decimal, such as 2.4. This represents the width of the rectangles in Set A and Set B.

In the second box, write a variable term, such as 3x.

In the third box, write a whole number that is less than 15, such as 5.

Step 2 Use the appropriate number of rectangles from Set A to represent the algebraic term in the second box. Arrange them to form a larger rectangle, C. Find the area of rectangle C.

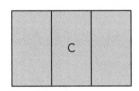

Area of rectangle C:
$(2.4)(3x) = 7.2x$

Step 3 Use the appropriate number of rectangles from Set B to represent the whole number in the third box. Arrange them to form a larger rectangle, D. Find the area of rectangle D.

Area of rectangle D:
$(2.4)(5) = 12$

Step 4 Arrange rectangles C and D to form a third rectangle, E. Add the two areas to find the total area of rectangle E.

Step 5 Record your results in the table on the Student Recording Sheet.

Step 6 Repeat Steps 1 to 5 at least four more times, using a different algebraic expression and a different decimal each time.

Step 7 Answer the questions on the Student Recording Sheet.

Lesson 3.4 Activity
Student Recording Sheet

Algebraic expression	Area of rectangle C	Area of rectangle D	Total area of rectangle E

1. What do you observe about the results you recorded in the table?

2. What conclusion can you draw from your observations?

Reflection

3. How can you use what you have learned about expanding algebraic expressions involving decimals that have two or more terms in parentheses?

Lesson 3.4 Activity
Materials

Set A

Lesson 3.4 Activity continued
Materials

Set B

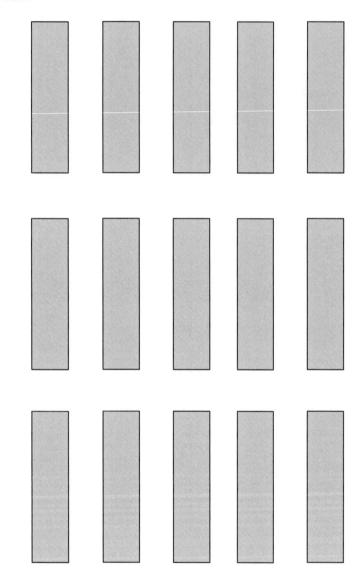

Lesson 3.6 Activity: Writing Algebraic Expressions

Teacher's Guide

Type of activity	Calculator activity
Objective	Reinforce the skills of writing and simplifying algebraic expressions.
Material	Calculator
Time	20–30 min
Ability levels	Mixed
Prerequisite skills	Multiply, divide, add, and subtract integers. Write and simplify algebraic expressions.
Grouping	Students should work in pairs or in small groups.
Assessment of students' learning	See Lesson 3.6 Activity: Rubric.

Lesson 3.6 Activity
Rubric

Category	4	3	2	1
Mathematical concepts	Explanation shows complete understanding of the mathematical concepts used to solve the problem(s).	Explanation shows substantial understanding of the mathematical concepts used to solve the problem(s).	Explanation shows some understanding of the mathematical concepts needed to solve the problem(s).	Explanation shows very limited understanding of the underlying concepts needed to solve the problem(s) OR is not written.
Reflection	The reflection shows clear thought and effort. The learning experience being reflected upon is relevant and meaningful to student and learning goals.	The reflection shows a lot of thought and effort. Student makes attempts to demonstrate relevance, but the relevance is unclear in reference to learning goals.	The reflection shows some thought and effort. Some sections of the reflection are irrelevant to student and/or learning goals.	The reflection is superficial. Most of the reflection is irrelevant to student and/or learning goals.

Lesson 3.6 Activity
Writing Algebraic Expressions

Step 1   Choose an integer that is greater than 10.

Step 2   Multiply the integer by 2.

Step 3   Subtract 3 from the result of Step 2.

Step 4   Divide the result of Step 3 by 4.

Step 5   Multiply the result of Step 4 by 12.

Step 6   Add 9 to the result of Step 5.

Step 7   Divide the result of Step 6 by 6. What is the final answer?

Step 8   Record your result in the table on the Student Recording Sheet.

Step 9   Repeat Steps 1 to 8 five times, starting with a different integer each time.

Step 10   Answer the questions about your results on the Student Recording Sheet.

Lesson 3.6 Activity
Student Recording Sheet

Integer (greater than 10)					
Multiply by 2					
Subtract 3					
Divide by 4					
Multiply by 12					
Add 9					
Divide by 6					
Final answer					

1. What do you notice about the results in the table?

2. Perform Steps 1 to 8 again, using the variable x in Step 1 instead of a number. Record your work in the table below, simplifying each expression. What conclusion can you draw?

Integer	x
Multiply by 2	
Subtract 3	
Divide by 4	
Multiply by 12	
Add 9	
Divide by 6	
Final answer	

Reflection

3. Explain why your conclusion is correct.

CHAPTER 3 Algebraic Expressions

Project: Factoring Algebraic Expressions

Teacher's Guide

Common Core State Standard	7.EE.1 Apply properties of operations as strategies to add, subtract, factor, and expand linear expressions with rational coefficients.
Objective	Reinforce the skill of factoring algebraic expressions.

Materials	• Two sets of shapes on pages 33 and 34:
	  – Use Set C (15 hexagons) to represent the first variable term.
	  – Use Set D (15 diamonds) to represent the second variable term.
	• Scissors

Time	20–30 min
Ability levels	Mixed
Prerequisite skill	Find the common factors of two whole numbers.
Grouping	Students should work in pairs or in small groups.
Assessment of students' learning	See Chapter 3 Project: Rubric.
Preparation	Give each group one set of hexagons and one set of diamonds.

Chapter 3 Project
Rubric

Category	4	3	2	1
Mathematical concepts	Explanation shows complete understanding of the mathematical concepts used to solve the problem(s).	Explanation shows substantial understanding of the mathematical concepts used to solve the problem(s).	Explanation shows some understanding of the mathematical concepts needed to solve the problem(s).	Explanation shows very limited understanding of the underlying concepts needed to solve the problem(s) OR is not written.
Mathematical reasoning	Uses complex and refined mathematical reasoning.	Uses effective mathematical reasoning.	Shows some evidence of mathematical reasoning.	Shows little evidence of mathematical reasoning.
Strategy/ Procedures	Uses an efficient and effective strategy to solve the problem(s).	Uses an effective strategy to solve the problem(s).	Uses an effective strategy to solve the problem(s) but does not do it consistently.	Does not use an effective strategy to solve the problem(s).
Working with others	Student was an engaged partner, listening to suggestions of others and working cooperatively throughout the lesson.	Student was an engaged partner but had trouble listening to others and/or working cooperatively.	Student cooperated with others, but needed prompting to stay on task.	Student did not work effectively with others.

Chapter 3 Project
Factoring Algebraic Expressions

In this project, you will explore factoring algebraic expressions involving the variables x and y. Use hexagons to represent the x-terms and diamonds to represent the y-terms.

Step 1   Using the first expression in the table below, arrange hexagons and diamonds to represent the expression.

Step 2   Rearrange the hexagons and diamonds into groups so that each group contains the same number of hexagons and diamonds.

Step 3   Repeat Steps 1 and 2 for each expression in the table. As you regroup each expression, think about these questions:

- How many groups are formed?
- How many hexagons and diamonds are there in each group?
- Is there more than one way of forming groups?
- What is the maximum number of groups that can be formed?

Algebraic expression	Maximum number of groups	Number of hexagons in each group	Number of diamonds in each group
4x + 6y	2	2	3
9x + 3y			
7x + 7y			
10x + 15y			
4x + 5y			
15x + 9y			
12x + 8y			

Step 4   Complete the table and answer the questions on the Student Recording Sheet. Summarize your findings and prepare a presentation to share with the class.

Chapter 3 Project
Student Recording Sheet

1. Write each algebraic expression in its factored form. Show your work.
An example is shown in the table.

Algebraic expression	First term	Second term	Greatest common factor	Factored form
$4x + 6y$	$4x$	$6y$	2	$4x + 6y = 2 \cdot 2x + 2 \cdot 3y$ $= 2(2x + 3y)$
$9x + 3y$				
$7x + 7y$				
$10x + 15y$				
$4x + 5y$				
$15x + 9y$				
$12x + 8y$				

2. Compare the table above with the one that you completed on the previous page. What do you notice?

3. Were there any rows for which you could not form equal groups of hexagons and diamonds? If yes, explain why.

Chapter 3 Project
Materials

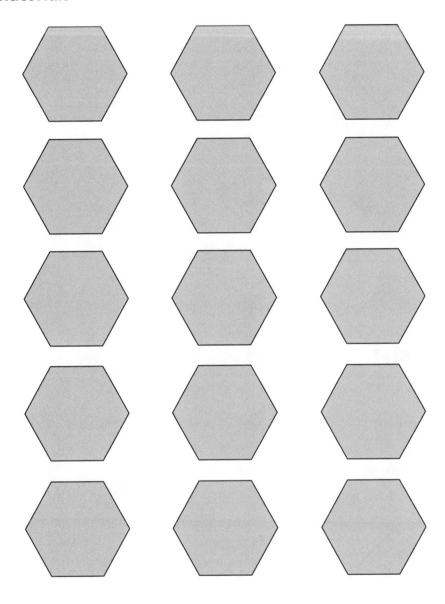

Chapter 3 Project continued
Materials

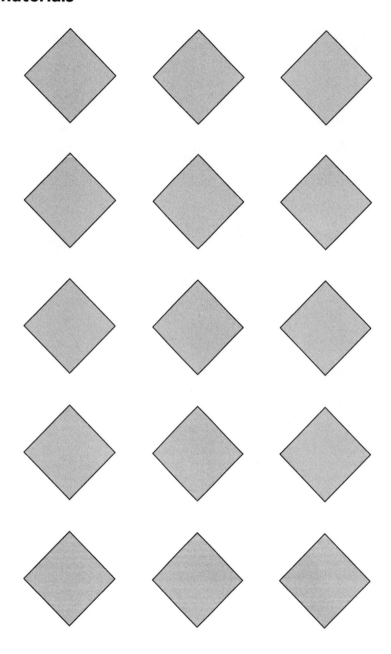

CHAPTER

Algebraic Equations and Inequalities

Lesson 4.1 Activity: Matching Equivalent Expressions

Teacher's Guide

Type of activity	Hands-on activity/game
Objective	Reinforce the skill of identifying equivalent expressions.
Materials	• Scissors • One set of the algebraic expression cards on pages 39 and 40 for each group
Time	20–30 min
Ability levels	Mixed
Prerequisite skills	Simplify and expand algebraic expressions.
Grouping	Students should work in pairs.
Assessment of students' learning	See Lesson 4.1 Activity: Rubric.

Lesson 4.1 Activity
Rubric

Category	4	3	2	1
Mathematical concepts	Explanation shows complete understanding of the mathematical concepts used to solve the problem(s).	Explanation shows substantial understanding of the mathematical concepts used to solve the problem(s).	Explanation shows some understanding of the mathematical concepts needed to solve the problem(s).	Explanation shows very limited understanding of the underlying concepts needed to solve the problem(s) OR is not written.
Self-assessment	Self-assessment is accurate and explanation is detailed and clear.	Self-assessment is fairly accurate and explanation is clear.	Self-assessment is inaccurate and explanation is a little difficult to understand, but includes critical components.	Self-assessment is totally inaccurate and explanation is difficult to understand and is missing several components OR is not included.
Reflection	The reflection shows clear thought and effort. The learning experience being reflected upon is relevant and meaningful to student and learning goals.	The reflection shows a lot of thought and effort. Student makes attempts to demonstrate relevance, but the relevance is unclear in reference to learning goals.	The reflection shows some thought and effort. Some sections of the reflection are irrelevant to student and/or learning goals.	The reflection is superficial. Most of the reflection is irrelevant to student and/or learning goals.

Lesson 4.1 Activity
Matching Equivalent Expressions

Step 1 Cut out the cards provided by your teacher.

Step 2 Shuffle the cards and place them face down on a desk or table.

Step 3 The first player will turn two of the cards face up. If the cards have equivalent expressions on them, the player keeps the cards. If they do not, turn the cards face down again, and the second player takes a turn.

Step 4 Record the equivalent expressions on the matching cards in the table on the Student Recording Sheet.

Step 5 Continue the game until all the expressions are matched correctly.

Step 6 The player with more pairs of equivalent expressions wins.

Lesson 4.1 Activity
Student Recording Sheet

Player 1		Player 2	
Equivalent expressions		Equivalent expressions	
Total score: _____		Total score: _____	

Self-Assessment and Reflection

1. In which skill(s) did you do well — simplifying algebraic expressions, expanding algebraic expressions, or identifying equivalent expressions? Explain.

2. In which skills(s) do you need more practice? Why do you think so?

3. What did you learn from this activity?

$3x - 7$	$2(y - 7x)$	$10x - 5$
$-5x + 2$	$xy + 12y$	$x(3 - y)$
$7 - 5(x + 1)$	$5x - 5 + 5x$	$y(-x + 1) + 6$
$2y - 14x$	$y(x + 12)$	$6x - 7 - 3x$

$-2xy + 3x + xy$	$-6 + 2(y + x)$	$\frac{1}{2}(-4y + 1)$
$y - \frac{21}{2}$	$\frac{1}{2}(x + y)$	$-2y + \frac{1}{2}$
$\frac{1}{3}(4x + y) - 1$	$-xy + 6 + y$	$y - (10 + \frac{1}{2})$
$\frac{1}{2}x + \frac{1}{2}y$	$2(x + y - 3)$	$\frac{4}{3}x + \frac{1}{3}y - 1$

Lessons 4.2 Activity: Algebraic Expressions and Equations

Teacher's Guide

Type of activity	Hands-on activity
Objective	Reinforce the skill of simplifying expressions and solving equations.
Material	Beads, counters, or other markers
Time	20–30 min
Ability levels	Mixed
Prerequisite skill	Divide a number by an integer.
Grouping	Students should work in groups of three.
Assessment of students' learning	See Lesson 4.2 Activity: Rubric.

Lessons 4.2 Activity
Rubric

Category	4	3	2	1
Mathematical concepts	Explanation shows complete understanding of the mathematical concepts used to solve the problem(s).	Explanation shows substantial understanding of the mathematical concepts used to solve the problem(s).	Explanation shows some understanding of the mathematical concepts needed to solve the problem(s).	Explanation shows very limited understanding of the underlying concepts needed to solve the problem(s) OR is not written.
Reflection	The reflection shows clear thought and effort. The learning experience being reflected upon is relevant and meaningful to student and learning goals.	The reflection shows a lot of thought and effort. Student makes attempts to demonstrate relevance, but the relevance is unclear in reference to learning goals.	The reflection shows some thought and effort. Some sections of the reflection are irrelevant to student and/or learning goals.	The reflection is superficial. Most of the reflection is irrelevant to student and/or learning goals.

Lesson 4.2 Activity
Algebraic Expressions and Equations

Mabel bought x beads. She keeps half of them for herself and shares the rest with two of her friends, Jess and Belle. Jess gets twice as many beads as Belle.

Let x represent the number of beads Mabel bought. The table shows the number of beads each of the girls will get.

Name	Number of beads
Mabel	$\frac{1}{2}x$
Jess	$\left(\frac{2}{3} \cdot \frac{1}{2}\right)x$
Belle	$\left(\frac{1}{3} \cdot \frac{1}{2}\right)x$

You can use beads or counters to find possible values of x.

Answer the questions on the Student Recording Sheet.

Lesson 4.2 Activity
Student Recording Sheet

1. Write an algebraic expression for the sum of the numbers of beads that all three girls have and show that it is equal to x.

2. Find three possible values of x.

3. What do you notice about the values of x?

4. Suppose you know that together, Mabel and Jess have 45 beads. Write an equation to find the number of beads that Mabel bought. Then solve your equation.

Reflection

5. Consider the following equation in which the variables a, b, and c, are integers. What are some possible values of a, b, and c?

$$\frac{1}{a} + \frac{1}{b} + \frac{1}{c} = 1$$

CHAPTER 4 Algebraic Equations and Inequalities

Project: Solving Algebraic Inequalities

Teacher's Guide

Common Core	
Common Core State Standard	7.EE.4b Solve word problems leading to inequalities of the form $px + q > r$ or $px + q < r$, where p, q, and r are specific rational numbers.
Objective	Reinforce the skill of solving algebraic inequalities.
Material	Calculator
Time	20–30 min
Ability levels	Mixed
Prerequisite skills	Add, subtract, multiply, and divide integers.
Grouping	Students should work in small groups.
Assessment of students' learning	See Chapter 4 Project: Rubric.

Chapter 4 Project
Rubric

Category	4	3	2	1
Mathematical concepts	Explanation shows complete understanding of the mathematical concepts used to solve the problem(s).	Explanation shows substantial understanding of the mathematical concepts used to solve the problem(s).	Explanation shows some understanding of the mathematical concepts needed to solve the problem(s).	Explanation shows very limited understanding of the underlying concepts needed to solve the problem(s) OR is not written.
Mathematical reasoning	Uses complex and refined mathematical reasoning.	Uses effective mathematical reasoning.	Shows some evidence of mathematical reasoning.	Shows little evidence of mathematical reasoning.
Strategy/ Procedures	Uses an efficient and effective strategy to solve the problem(s).	Uses an effective strategy to solve the problem(s).	Uses an effective strategy to solve the problem(s) but does not do it consistently.	Does not use a effective strategy to solve the problem(s).
Working with others	Student was an engaged partner, listening to suggestions of others and working cooperatively throughout the lesson.	Student was an engaged partner but had trouble listening to others and/or working cooperatively.	Student cooperated with others, but needed prompting to stay on task.	Student did not work effectively with others.

Chapter 4 Project
Solving Algebraic Inequalities

There are 25 students in a class. Nicole, the school administrator, has a budget of $400 to pay for a field trip for the class. The table below shows cost information for transportation and food from some companies that Nicole can use for the field trip. Each company also charges a service fee of $50.

	Cost of transportation (x dollars)	Cost of food (y dollars)
Company A	$7 per passenger	$10 per passenger (includes food and drink)
Company B	$10 for the first 20 passengers and $5 for subsequent passenger	$5 per passenger (additional $2 for each drink)
Company C	$15 per passenger	$8 per passenger (no drinks included)
Company D	$12 for the first 10 passengers and $8 for subsequent passenger	$5 per passenger (no drinks included)
Company E	$10 per passenger	$8 per passenger (includes food and drink)

For this project, you will use inequalities to help Nicole choose the most cost-effective company or companies to use for the field trip.

Answer the questions on the Student Recording Sheet.

Chapter 4 Project
Student Recording Sheet

1. Write an expression in terms of x and y to express the total amount of money to be spent on the class field trip. Then write an inequality using your expression.

2. Which company do you think Nicole should choose for the class field trip so that it is within the budget? Explain your choice.

5 Direct and Inverse Proportion

Lesson 5.1 Activity: Direct Proportion

Teacher's Guide

Type of activity	Hands-on activity
Objective	Reinforce the concept of direct proportion.
Materials	• Square grid on page 53 • Rectangles on page 54 • Scissors
Time	20–30 min
Ability levels	Mixed
Prerequisite skill	Multiply integers.
Grouping	Students should work in pairs.
Assessment of students' learning	See Lesson 5.1 Activity: Rubric.

Lesson 5.1 Activity
Rubric

Category	4	3	2	1
Mathematical concepts	Explanation shows complete understanding of the mathematical concepts used to solve the problem(s).	Explanation shows substantial understanding of the mathematical concepts used to solve the problem(s).	Explanation shows some understanding of the mathematical concepts needed to solve the problem(s).	Explanation shows very limited understanding of the underlying concepts needed to solve the problem(s) OR is not written.
Reflection	The reflection shows clear thought and effort. The learning experience being reflected upon is relevant and meaningful to student and learning goals.	The reflection shows a lot of thought and effort. Student makes attempts to demonstrate relevance, but the relevance is unclear in reference to learning goals.	The reflection shows some thought and effort. Some sections of the reflection are irrelevant to student and/or learning goals.	The reflection is superficial. Most of the reflection is irrelevant to student and/or learning goals.

Lesson 5.1 Activity
Direct Proportion

Step 1   Cut out the squares on page 53.

Step 2   Choose a rectangle on page 54.

Step 3   Arrange enough squares to cover the rectangle with no gaps or overlapping squares.

Step 4   Count the number of squares that fit the vertical side (*v*) and the horizontal side (*h*) of the rectangle respectively. Then find the area of the rectangle in terms of the number of squares that you used.

Step 5   Record your results in the table on the Student Recording Sheet.

Step 6   Repeat Steps 2 to 5 for the remaining rectangles on page 54.

Step 7   Answer the questions on the Student Recording Sheet.

Lesson 5.1 Activity
Student Recording Sheet

Number of squares on the vertical side, v	Number of squares on the horizontal side, h	Area of the rectangle, A square units

1. What do you notice about the values of v in the table?

2. Write an equation that expresses the relationship between v, h, and A.

3. Describe the relationship between A and h.

Reflection

4. Which two variables in this activity are in direct proportion? Why?

Lesson 5.1 Activity
Materials

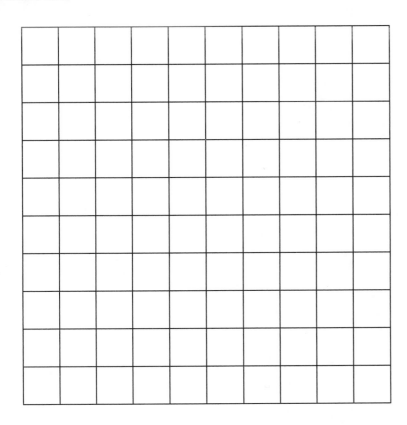

Lesson 5.1 Activity continued
Materials

CHAPTER 5   Direct and Inverse Proportion

Project: Decorating Boards

Teacher's Guide

Common Core **Common Core State Standard**	7.RP.2a Decide whether two quantities are in a proportional relationship…
Objective	Reinforce the concept of inverse proportion.
Materials	• Measuring tape • Stickers on page 60 • Scissors • String
Time	20–30 min
Ability levels	Advanced
Prerequisite skills	Divide integers. Understand direct and inverse proportion. Graph points on a coordinate plane.
Grouping	Students should work in pairs.
Assessment of students' learning	See Chapter 5 Project: Rubric.
Preparation	In this project, students will count the number of stickers that can be placed along one side of a bulletin board chosen by the teacher. The number of stickers depends on the length of the chosen board. Make as many copies of the stickers as necessary. If students are not able to measure the length of a bulletin board, give them an appropriate length of string to use in Step 1 of the project.

Chapter 5 Project
Rubric

Category	4	3	2	1
Mathematical concepts	Explanation shows complete understanding of the mathematical concepts used to solve the problem(s).	Explanation shows substantial understanding of the mathematical concepts used to solve the problem(s).	Explanation shows some understanding of the mathematical concepts needed to solve the problem(s).	Explanation shows very limited understanding of the underlying concepts needed to solve the problem(s) OR is not written.
Neatness and organization	The work is presented in a neat, clear, organized fashion that is easy to read.	The work is presented in a neat and organized fashion that is usually easy to read.	The work is presented in an organized fashion but may be hard to read at times.	The work appears sloppy and unorganized. It is hard to know what information goes together.
Strategy/ Procedures	Typically uses an efficient and effective strategy to solve the problem(s).	Typically uses an effective strategy to solve the problem(s).	Sometimes uses an effective strategy to solve problems, but does not do so consistently.	Rarely uses an effective strategy to solve problems.
Presentation	Presentation of mathematical calculations is detailed and clear.	Presentation of mathematical calculations is clear.	Presentation of mathematical calculations is a little difficult to understand, but includes critical components.	Presentation of mathematical calculations is difficult to understand and is missing several components OR is not included.

Chapter 5 Project
Decorating Boards

Suppose your teacher has asked you to decorate the top of a bulletin board with stickers. The stickers have to be evenly spaced. You have to decide how many stickers you need.

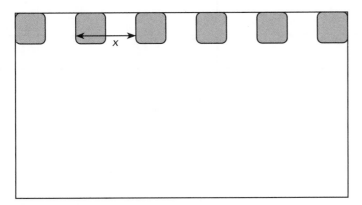

Step 1   Use a measuring tape to measure the length of the bulletin board that your teacher chooses. Cut a piece of string the same length.

Step 2   Using a distance of 1 inch between two stickers, arrange the stickers along the length of string. Measure the distance from the left edge of one sticker to the same point on the next sticker. This distance is x.

Step 3   Count the number of stickers on the string. This number is y.

Step 4   Record your data in the table on the Student Recording Sheet.

Step 5   Repeat Steps 2 to 4 at least four times, using a different distance between the stickers each time.

Step 6   Using the data from the table, plot the points on the graph on the Student Recording Sheet and connect the points. Then answer the questions on the Student Recording Sheet.

Step 7   Summarize your findings and prepare a simple presentation to share in class.

Chapter 5 Project
Student Recording Sheet

Length of bulletin board					
Distance between edges of two stickers, x	1	2	3	4	5
Number of stickers, y					

Using a suitable scale for the vertical axis, graph the relationship between x and y.

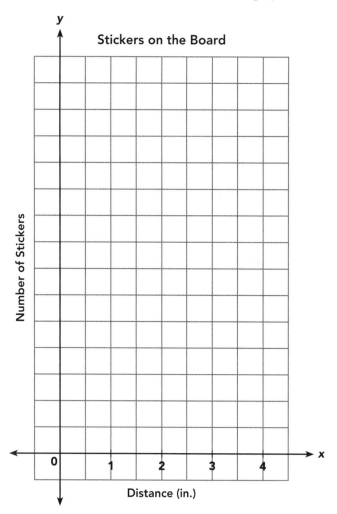

Stickers on the Board

Chapter 5 Project continued
Student Recording Sheet

1. Tell whether the graph represents a *direct* proportion or an *inverse* proportion.

2. Find the constant of proportionality for your graph.

3. Write an equation that relates x and y.

4. Select a point on the graph and explain what the coordinates of the point represent.

Chapter 5 Project
Materials

6 Angle Properties and Straight Lines

Lesson 6.1 Activity: Identifying Complementary and Supplementary Angles

Teacher's Guide

Type of activity	Hands-on activity
Objective	Reinforce the concepts of complementary angles and supplementary angles.
Materials	• Protractor • Ruler
Time	20–30 min
Ability levels	Mixed
Prerequisite skill	Measure angles with a protractor.
Grouping	Students should work in pairs.
Assessment of students' learning	See Lesson 6.1 Activity: Rubric.

Lesson 6.1 Activity
Rubric

Category	4	3	2	1
Mathematical concepts	Explanation shows complete understanding of the mathematical concepts used to solve the problem(s).	Explanation shows substantial understanding of the mathematical concepts used to solve the problem(s).	Explanation shows some understanding of the mathematical concepts needed to solve the problem(s).	Explanation shows very limited understanding of the underlying concepts needed to solve the problem(s) OR is not written.
Reflection	The reflection shows clear thought and effort. The learning experience being reflected upon is relevant and meaningful to student and learning goals.	The reflection shows a lot of thought and effort. Student makes attempts to demonstrate relevance, but the relevance is unclear in reference to learning goals.	The reflection shows some thought and effort. Some sections of the reflection are irrelevant to student and/or learning goals.	The reflection is superficial. Most of the reflection is irrelevant to student and/or learning goals.

Lesson 6.1 Activity
Identifying Complementary and Supplementary Angles

Step 1   Measure the angles in the quadrilateral on the Student Recording Sheet with a protractor. Write the angle measures on the diagram.

Step 2   Identify pairs of complementary angles in the diagram.

Step 3   Identify pairs of adjacent supplementary angles on a straight line in the diagram.

Step 4   Record your data in the table on the Student Recording Sheet. An example is shown in the table.

Complementary angles	$\angle HAK$ and $\angle KAB$ $60° + 30°$ $= 90°$
Supplementary angles	$\angle GKA$ and $\angle AKC$ $(30° + 30°) + (60° + 60°)$ $= 60° + 120°$ $= 180°$

Name: _____   Date: _____

Lesson 6.1 Activity
Student Recording Sheet

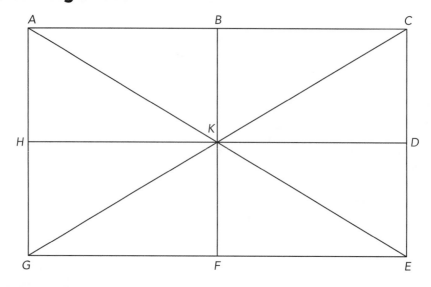

Complementary angles	
Supplementary angles	

Reflection

Write at least three different conclusions about angle measures that you could make from this activity.

Lessons 6.2–6.3 Activity: Identifying Congruent Angles

Teacher's Guide

Type of activity	Hands-on activity
Objective	Reinforce the concepts of vertical angles and alternate angles.
Materials	• Ruler • Protractor
Time	20–30 min
Ability levels	Mixed
Prerequisite skills	Measure angles with a protractor. Apply the properties of parallelograms.
Grouping	Students should work in pairs.
Assessment of students' learning	See Lessons 6.2–6.3 Activity: Rubric.

Lessons 6.2–6.3 Activity
Rubric

Category	4	3	2	1
Mathematical concepts	Explanation shows complete understanding of the mathematical concepts used to solve the problem(s).	Explanation shows substantial understanding of the mathematical concepts used to solve the problem(s).	Explanation shows some understanding of the mathematical concepts needed to solve the problem(s).	Explanation shows very limited understanding of the underlying concepts needed to solve the problem(s) OR is not written.
Reflection	The reflection shows clear thought and effort. The learning experience being reflected upon is relevant and meaningful to student and learning goals.	The reflection shows a lot of thought and effort. Student makes attempts to demonstrate relevance, but the relevance is unclear in reference to learning goals.	The reflection shows some thought and effort. Some sections of the reflection are irrelevant to student and/or learning goals	The reflection is superficial. Most of the reflection is irrelevant to student and/or learning goals.

Lessons 6.2–6.3 Activity
Identifying Congruent Angles

For each quadrilateral given:

Step 1   Identify the type of quadrilateral and label its vertices.

Step 2   Use a ruler to connect each pair of opposite vertices of the quadrilateral to form the two diagonals.

Step 3   Identify the pairs of alternate interior angles and vertical angles created by the diagonals and sides of the quadrilateral.

Step 4   Use a protractor to find the measure of each pair of angles that you listed in Step 3.

Step 5   Record your data in the tables on the Student Recording Sheet.

Name: _____ Date: _____

Lessons 6.2–6.3 Activity
Student Recording Sheet

Type of quadrilateral: _____

Angle pairs	Angle property

Type of quadrilateral: _____

Angle pairs	Angle property

Name: _____   Date: _____

Lessons 6.2–6.3 Activity continued
Student Recording Sheet

Type of quadrilateral: _____	
Angle pairs	**Angle property**

Type of quadrilateral: _____	
Angle pairs	**Angle property**

Lessons 6.2–6.3 Activity continued
Student Recording Sheet

Answer these questions.

1. Record the number of pairs of congruent angles in the table below.

Quadrilateral	Number of pairs of congruent angles

2. What types of quadrilaterals listed in the table have the same number of pairs of congruent angles?

3. What properties do the quadrilaterals listed in Question 2 have in common?

Reflection

4. What can you conclude from this activity?

CHAPTER 6   Angle Properties and Straight Lines

Project: Interior and Exterior Angles

Teacher's Guide

Common Core	
Common Core State Standard	8.G.5 Use informal arguments to establish facts about the angle sum and exterior angle of triangles.
Objective	Reinforce the concepts of interior and exterior angles.
Materials	• Ruler • Protractor
Time	20–30 min
Ability levels	Advanced
Prerequisite skills	Measure angles and add their measures. Understand the properties of quadrilaterals, pentagons, and hexagons.
Grouping	Students should work in pairs.
Assessment of students' learning	See Chapter 6 Project: Rubric.

Chapter 6 Project
Rubric

Category	4	3	2	1
Mathematical concepts	Explanation shows complete understanding of the mathematical concepts used to solve the problem(s).	Explanation shows substantial understanding of the mathematical concepts used to solve the problem(s).	Explanation shows some understanding of the mathematical concepts needed to solve the problem(s).	Explanation shows very limited understanding of the underlying concepts needed to solve the problem(s) OR is not written.
Mathematical reasoning	Uses complex and refined mathematical reasoning.	Uses effective mathematical reasoning.	Shows some evidence of mathematical reasoning.	Shows little evidence of mathematical reasoning.
Working with others	Student was an engaged partner, listening to suggestions of others and working cooperatively throughout the lesson.	Student was an engaged partner but had trouble listening to others and/or working cooperatively.	Student cooperated with others, but needed prompting to stay on task.	Student did not work effectively with others.
Explanation	Explanation is detailed and clear.	Explanation is clear.	Explanation is a little difficult to understand, but includes critical components.	Explanation is difficult to understand and is missing several components OR is not included.

Chapter 6 Project
Interior and Exterior Angles

Step 1   Draw a triangle.

Step 2   Measure its interior angles with a protractor. Find the sum of the measures and record it in the table on the Student Recording Sheet.

Step 3   Extend each side of the triangle in one direction.

Step 4   Measure each *exterior angle* formed by extending the sides. Find the sum of the three measures and record it in the table on the Student Recording Sheet.

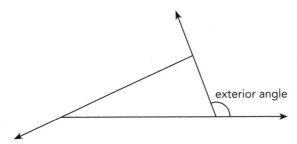

exterior angle

Step 5   Repeat Steps 1 to 4, using a quadrilateral, a pentagon, and a hexagon instead of a triangle.

Step 6   Answer the questions on the Student Recording Sheet.

Chapter 6 Project
Student Recording Sheet

Polygon	Number of sides	Sum of interior angles	Sum of exterior angles	Total sum
Triangle				
Quadrilateral				
Pentagon				
Hexagon				

Show your work.

1. What is the sum of the measures of all the exterior angles in any polygon?

2. What is the sum of the measures of all the interior and exterior angles in a polygon with *n* sides?

3. What is the sum of the measures of the interior angles in a polygon with *n* sides? Justify your answer.

Geometric Construction

Lessons 7.1–7.3 Activity: Inscribed and Circumscribed Circles of a Triangle

Teacher's Guide

Type of activity	Hands-on activity
Objective	Reinforce the skills of constructing angle and perpendicular bisectors.
Materials	• Compass • Ruler
Time	20–30 min
Ability levels	Mixed
Prerequisite skill	Draw a circle with a compass.
Grouping	Students should work alone or in pairs.
Assessment of students' learning	See Lessons 7.1–7.3 Activity: Rubric.

Lessons 7.1–7.3 Activity Rubric

Category	4	3	2	1
Mathematical concepts	Explanation shows complete understanding of the mathematical concepts used to solve the problem(s).	Explanation shows substantial understanding of the mathematical concepts used to solve the problem(s).	Explanation shows some understanding of the mathematical concepts needed to solve the problem(s).	Explanation shows very limited understanding of the underlying concepts needed to solve the problem(s) OR is not written.
Reflection	The reflection shows clear thought and effort. The learning experience being reflected upon is relevant and meaningful to student and learning goals.	The reflection shows a lot of thought and effort. Student makes attempts to demonstrate relevance, but the relevance is unclear in reference to learning goals.	The reflection shows some thought and effort. Some sections of the reflection are irrelevant to student and/or learning goals.	The reflection is superficial. Most of the reflection is irrelevant to student and/or learning goals.

Name: _____   Date: _____

Lessons 7.1–7.3 Activity
Inscribed and Circumscribed Circles of a Triangle

Step 1   Use a compass and ruler to draw a triangle with sides measuring 6 inches, 8 inches, and 10 inches. Identify the type of triangle you have drawn.

Step 2   Construct the angle bisectors of each angle in the triangle.

Step 3   Using the point where the angle bisectors intersect as a center, draw a circle that touches each side of the triangle. This circle is called the *inscribed circle* of the triangle.

Step 4   Construct the perpendicular bisectors of each side of the triangle.

Step 5   Using the point where the perpendicular bisectors intersect as a center, draw a circle that passes through all the vertices of the triangle. This circle is called the *circumscribed circle* of the triangle.

Step 6   Answer the questions on the Student Recording Sheet.

Lessons 7.1–7.3 Activity
Student Recording Sheet

1. Identify the type of triangle you have drawn.

2. Find the radius of the inscribed circle.

3. Find the radius of the circumscribed circle. What do you notice about the radius?

4. Do the inscribed circle and the circumscribed circle have the same center?

Reflection

5. Draw several different triangles, including some scalene, isosceles, and equilateral triangles. Using Steps 2 to 5, draw the inscribed and circumscribed circles of each triangle.
   a) Do all the triangles have an inscribed circle and a circumscribed circle?

   b) For some triangles, the inscribed circle and the circumscribed circle have the same center. What type of triangle has this property?

CHAPTER 7   Geometric Construction

Project: Cyclic Quadrilateral

Teacher's Guide

Common Core (logo)	
Common Core State Standard	7.G.2 Draw (freehand, with ruler and protractor, and with technology) geometric shapes with given conditions. G-C.3 . . . [P]rove properties of angles for a quadrilateral inscribed in a circle.
Objective	Draw conclusions about the angles of a quadrilateral inscribed in a circle.
Materials	• Compass • Ruler • Protractor • Alternatively, use geometry drawing software.
Time	20–30 min
Ability levels	Mixed
Prerequisite skills	Measure an angle with a protractor. Draw an angle with a protractor. Draw a circle with a compass.
Grouping	Students should work in pairs or in small groups.
Assessment of students' learning	See Chapter 7 Project: Rubric.

Chapter 7 Project
Rubric

Category	4	3	2	1
Mathematical concepts	Explanation shows complete understanding of the mathematical concepts used to solve the problem(s).	Explanation shows substantial understanding of the mathematical concepts used to solve the problem(s).	Explanation shows some understanding of the mathematical concepts needed to solve the problem(s).	Explanation shows very limited understanding of the underlying concepts needed to solve the problem(s) OR is not written.
Mathematical reasoning	Uses complex and refined mathematical reasoning.	Uses effective mathematical reasoning.	Shows some evidence of mathematical reasoning.	Shows little evidence of mathematical reasoning.
Explanation	Explanation is detailed and clear.	Explanation is clear.	Explanation is a little difficult to understand, but includes critical components.	Explanation is difficult to understand and is missing several components OR is not included.
Working with others	Student was an engaged partner, listening to suggestions of others and working cooperatively throughout the lesson.	Student was an engaged partner but had trouble listening to others and/or working cooperatively.	Student cooperated with others, but needed prompting to stay on task.	Student did not work effectively with others.

Chapter 7 Project
Cyclic Quadrilateral

A cyclic quadrilateral is a quadrilateral inscribed in a circle, where all the vertices of the quadrilateral lie on the circumference of the circle. In this activity, you will explore the properties of angles in a cyclic quadrilateral.

Step 1   Use a compass to draw a circle.

Step 2   Choose points *A*, *B*, *C*, and *D* on the circumference of the circle and use a straightedge to draw quadrilateral *ABCD*.

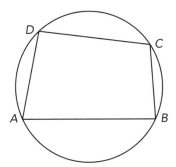

Step 3   Use a protractor to measure the angles of the quadrilateral. Record your results in the table on the Student Recording Sheet.

Step 4   Repeat Steps 1 to 3 at least three more times.

Step 5   Look at the results for your quadrilaterals. What do you notice about the measures of the angles?

Step 6   Answer the questions on the Student Recording Sheet.

Name: _____   Date: _____

Chapter 7 Project
Student Recording Sheet

Quadrilateral	m∠A	m∠B	m∠C	m∠D
1				
2				
3				
4				

1. What do you notice about the angles of the quadrilateral? Make a conclusion about the angles of a quadrilateral inscribed in a circle.

2. Draw an example of a quadrilateral that cannot be inscribed in a circle.

Volume and Surface Area of Solids

Lessons 8.2–8.4 Activity: Finding the Maximum Volume

Teacher's Guide

Type of activity	Hands-on activity
Objective	Reinforce the skill of finding volume of solids.
Materials	<ul><li>Nets of cube, cylinder, cone, and sphere on pages 87 to 90</li><li>Scissors</li><li>Sticky tape</li><li>Ruler</li></ul>
Time	20–30 min
Ability levels	Mixed
Prerequisite skill	Multiply fractions.
Grouping	Students should work in pairs.
Assessment of students' learning	See Lessons 8.2–8.4 Activity: Rubric.

Lessons 8.2–8.4 Activity Rubric

Category	4	3	2	1
Mathematical concepts	Explanation shows complete understanding of the mathematical concepts used to solve the problem(s).	Explanation shows substantial understanding of the mathematical concepts used to solve the problem(s).	Explanation shows some understanding of the mathematical concepts needed to solve the problem(s).	Explanation shows very limited understanding of the underlying concepts needed to solve the problem(s) OR is not written.
Reflection	The reflection shows clear thought and effort. The learning experience being reflected upon is relevant and meaningful to student and learning goals.	The reflection shows a lot of thought and effort. Student makes attempts to demonstrate relevance, but the relevance is unclear in reference to learning goals.	The reflection shows some thought and effort. Some sections of the reflection is irrelevant to student and/or learning goals.	The reflection is superficial. Most of the reflection is irrelevant to student and/or learning goals.

Lessons 8.2–8.4 Activity
Finding the Maximum Volume

Suppose you are the product designer for an ornament manufacturer. Your job is to choose a three-dimensional ornament, preferably with the largest possible volume, to fit in a box. The box is a cube with edges 2 inches.

Step 1   Cut out the net of the cube. Fold and tape the net to form a box.

Step 2   Select a shape from the nets provided.

Step 3   Cut out the selected net. Fold and tape the net to form the solid.

Step 4   Put your solid into the box.

Step 5   Answer the questions on the Student Recording Sheet.

At the end of the activity, return the solid shapes to your teacher. You will use them for the Chapter 8 Project.

Lessons 8.2–8.4 Activity
Student Recording Sheet

1. What is the volume of the box?

2. Which solid did you select? Give a reason for your choice.

3. Find the volume of the solid that you chose. Use a ruler to find the appropriate dimensions.

Solid	Formula	Volume
Cylinder	$\pi r^2 h$	
Cone	$\frac{1}{3}\pi r^2 h$	
Sphere	$\frac{4}{3}\pi r^3$	

Reflection

4. Compare the volume of the solid that you chose with the volume of the box. Do you think that you chose the solid with the closest fit? Explain.

CHAPTER 8 Volume and Surface Area of Solids

Project: Finding the Minimum Surface Area

Teacher's Guide

Common Core State Standard	7.G.6 Solve real-world and mathematical problems involving area, volume and surface area of two- and three-dimensional objects composed of triangles, quadrilaterals, polygons, cubes, and right prisms.
Objective	Reinforce the skill of finding surface area of solids.
Material	• Solids made in Lessons 8.2–8.4 Activity • Ruler
Time	20–30 min
Ability levels	Mixed
Prerequisite skill	Multiply fractions.
Grouping	Students should work in small groups.
Assessment of students' learning	See Chapter 8 Project: Rubric.
Preparation	Sort the solids that students made in Lessons 8.2–8.4 Activity. If necessary, prepare more solids such that each group of students will get a cube, a cone, a sphere, and a cylinder.

Chapter 8 Project
Rubric

Category	4	3	2	1
Mathematical concepts	Explanation shows complete understanding of the mathematical concepts used to solve the problem(s).	Explanation shows substantial understanding of the mathematical concepts used to solve the problem(s).	Explanation shows some understanding of the mathematical concepts needed to solve the problem(s).	Explanation shows very limited understanding of the underlying concepts needed to solve the problem(s) OR is not written.
Mathematical reasoning	Uses complex and refined mathematical reasoning.	Uses effective mathematical reasoning.	Shows some evidence of mathematical reasoning.	Shows little evidence of mathematical reasoning.
Strategy/ Procedures	Uses an efficient and effective strategy to solve the problem(s).	Uses an effective strategy to solve the problem(s).	Uses an effective strategy to solve the problem(s) but does not do it consistently.	Does not use an effective strategy to solve the problem(s).
Working with others	Student was an engaged partner, listening to suggestions of others and working cooperatively throughout the lesson.	Student was an engaged partner but had trouble listening to others and/or working cooperatively.	Student cooperated with others, but needed prompting to stay on task.	Student did not work effectively with others.

CHAPTER

Statistics

Lesson 9.4 Activity: Random Sampling

Teacher's Guide

Type of activity	Hands-on activity
Objective	Reinforce the understanding of random sampling.
Materials	• Measuring tape • List of names of 24 students • Number cube with sides numbered 1 through 6
Time	20–30 min
Ability levels	Mixed
Prerequisite skill	Find the mean of a set of data.
Grouping	Students should work in pairs.
Assessment of students' learning	See Lesson 9.4 Activity: Rubric.
Preparation	In this activity, students will use the heights of 24 students as a data set. If there is not enough time to measure the students' heights in class, you can measure the heights of the students before class and prepare a list of the heights for use in the activity.

Lesson 9.4 Activity
Rubric

Category	4	3	2	1
Mathematical concepts	Explanation shows complete understanding of the mathematical concepts used to solve the problem(s).	Explanation shows substantial understanding of the mathematical concepts used to solve the problem(s).	Explanation shows some understanding of the mathematical concepts needed to solve the problem(s).	Explanation shows very limited understanding of the underlying concepts needed to solve the problem(s) OR is not written.
Reflection	The reflection shows clear thought and effort. The learning experience being reflected upon is relevant and meaningful to student and learning goals.	The reflection shows a lot of thought and effort. Student makes attempts to demonstrate relevance, but the relevance is unclear in reference to learning goals.	The reflection shows some thought and effort. Some sections of the reflection are irrelevant to student and/or learning goals.	The reflection is superficial. Most of the reflection is irrelevant to student and/or learning goals.

Lesson 9.4 Activity
Random Sampling

Step 1   You will use a list of 24 students. Measure and record the heights of all the students on the list. This list will be used later in the activity.

Step 2   Choose a random sample from the list of 24 students using the following method:

For each student on the list, roll a number cube. If the number you rolled is 1 or 2, write the student's name and height in the table on the Student Recording Sheet. If the number rolled is 3 or greater, go to the next name on the list. Continue until you have rolled the number cube for each student.

Step 3   Answer the questions on the Student Recording Sheet.

Lesson 9.4 Activity
Student Recording Sheet

	Name of Student	Height (in.)		Name of Student	Height (in.)
1			6		
2			7		
3			8		
4			9		
5			10		

1. Find the mean height of the students in the sample.

2. Find the mean height of the 24 students in the population.

3. Compare the mean height of the students in the sample to the mean height of the 24 students. What do you notice?

Reflection

4. Suppose you increased the number of students in the sample. How do you think the mean of the heights of the students in the sample would be affected?

Lesson 9.5 Activity
Making a Prediction

Teacher's Guide

Types of activity	Hands-on activity
Objective	Reinforce the understanding of making inferences about populations.
Materials	• Beads, counters, markers, or slips of paper that are identical in size and shape, but in two different colors. You will need at least 70 of each color. • Paper or fabric bag
Time	20–30 min
Ability levels	Mixed
Prerequisite skills	Multiply and divide integers. Find the mean of a set of data.
Grouping	Students should work in small groups.
Assessment of students' learning	See Lesson 9.5 Activity: Rubric.
Preparation	Select some counters of each color, so that there is a total of 100 counters. Place the 100 counters in the bag. Do not let students know how many counters of each color are in the bag.

Lesson 9.5 Activity
Rubric

Category	4	3	2	1
Mathematical concepts	Explanation shows complete understanding of the mathematical concepts used to solve the problem(s).	Explanation shows substantial understanding of the mathematical concepts used to solve the problem(s).	Explanation shows some understanding of the mathematical concepts needed to solve the problem(s).	Explanation shows very limited understanding of the underlying concepts needed to solve the problem(s) OR is not written.
Mathematical reasoning	Uses complex and refined mathematical reasoning.	Uses effective mathematical reasoning.	Shows some evidence of mathematical reasoning.	Shows little evidence of mathematical reasoning.
Working with others	Student was an engaged partner, listening to suggestions of others and working cooperatively throughout the lesson.	Student was an engaged partner but had trouble listening to others and/or working cooperatively.	Student cooperated with others, but needed prompting to stay on task.	Student did not work effectively with others.
Reflection	The reflection shows clear thought and effort. The learning experience being reflected upon is relevant and meaningful to student and learning goals.	The reflection shows a lot of thought and effort. Student makes attempts to demonstrate relevance, but the relevance is unclear in reference to learning goals.	The reflection shows some thought and effort. Some sections of the reflection are irrelevant to student and/or learning goals.	The reflection is superficial. Most of the reflection is irrelevant to student and/or learning goals.

Chapter 9.5 Activity
Making a Prediction

You will use a bag filled with counters or beads of two different colors.

Step 1   Without looking, draw a sample of 10 counters from the bag.

Step 2   Count the number of one color, Color A, of the counters that you have drawn.

Step 3   Record the number you found in Step 2 in the table on the Student Recording Sheet.

Step 4   Return the 10 counters to the bag and shake the bag.

Step 5   Repeat Steps 1 to 4 a total of ten times.

Step 6   Answer the questions on the Student Recording Sheet.

Lesson 9.5 Activity
Student Recording Sheet

Sample	1	2	3	4	5	6	7	8	9	10
Number of Color A counters in the sample										

1. What is the mean of the numbers from the 10 samples?

2. Find the ratio $\dfrac{\text{Mean of the number of Color A counters}}{\text{Number of counters drawn in each round}}$ for a sample size of 10 counters.

3. Using the ratio in Question 2, estimate the number of Color A counters in a sample size of 100 counters.

4. Count the Color A counters in the bag and compare your result with the estimate you found in Question 3. What do you notice?

Reflection

5. What have you learned from this activity? Can you think of a situation where this method of estimating a number could be used in real life?

CHAPTER 9 Statistics

Project: Letter Frequency

Teacher's Guide

Common Core State Standards	7.SP.1 Understand that statistics can be used to gain information about a population by examining a sample of the population; generalizations about a population from a sample are valid only if the sample is representative of that population. Understand that random sampling tends to produce representative samples and support valid inferences.
Objective	Reinforce the understanding that random sampling can be used to make a generalization about a population.
Material	A 150–200 word extract from an article or essay
Time	30 min
Ability levels	Mixed
Prerequisite skills	Multiply and divide integers.
Grouping	Students should work in groups of three.
Assessment of students' learning	See Chapter 9 Project: Rubric.
Preparation	Ask each group to bring to class articles from newspapers or magazines. They can also use their own essays for this task. Each member of the group should have a copy of the article or essay. Search online for the theoretical frequency of letters of the alphabet. Print a copy for each group to be used later for comparison with their collected data.

Chapter 9 Project
Rubric

Category	4	3	2	1
Mathematical concepts	Explanation shows complete understanding of the mathematical concepts used to solve the problem(s).	Explanation shows substantial understanding of the mathematical concepts used to solve the problem(s).	Explanation shows some understanding of the mathematical concepts needed to solve the problem(s).	Explanation shows very limited understanding of the underlying concepts needed to solve the problem(s) OR is not written.
Mathematical reasoning	Uses complex and refined mathematical reasoning.	Uses effective mathematical reasoning.	Shows some evidence of mathematical reasoning.	Shows little evidence of mathematical reasoning.
Strategy/ Procedures	Uses an efficient and effective strategy to solve the problem(s).	Uses an effective strategy to solve the problem(s).	Uses an effective strategy to solve the problem(s), but does not do it consistently.	Does not use an effective strategy to solve the problem(s).
Working with others	Student was an engaged partner, listening to suggestions of others and working cooperatively throughout the lesson.	Student was an engaged partner but had trouble listening to others and/or working cooperatively.	Student cooperated with others, but needed prompting to stay on task.	Student did not work effectively with others.

Chapter 9 Project
Letter Frequency

In this project, your group will examine an extract from an article and determine the frequency of each vowel (A, E, I, O, and U) in the extract. Which vowel do you think will have the highest frequency?

Step 1   Select an extract of about 150 to 200 words from your article.

Step 2   Count the total number of letters in the extract. Then count the number of each vowel in the extract. Record the results in the table on the Student Recording Sheet.

Step 3   Find the frequency of each vowel, in percent, using
$$\frac{\text{Number of the vowel}}{\text{Total number of letters}} \cdot 100\%.$$ Round the answer to the nearest hundredth. Complete the table on the Student Recording Sheet.

Step 4   Compare your results with the theoretical frequency of letters of the alphabet your teacher has given you. Are the results what you expected?

Step 5   Compare your results with the rest of the class. Are your results similar to the results of other groups?

Step 6   Answer the questions on the Student Recording Sheet. Summarize your findings and prepare a short presentation to share in class.

Name: _____   Date: _____

Chapter 9 Project
Student Recording Sheet

Total number of letters in the extract = _____

Vowel	A	E	I	O	U	Total
Frequency						
Frequency (%)						

1. Based on your data, which vowel has the highest frequency? _____

2. Ask the other groups for the frequency in their extracts of the vowel you identified in Question 1. Record the results in the table below. Arrange the frequencies in order from least to greatest.

Group										
Frequency of the vowel ___										

3. In the space below, draw a box plot for the data and label it with the 5-point summary.

Q_1 = _____ Q_2 = _____ Q_3 = _____

Lower extreme value = _____   Upper extreme value = _____

CHAPTER

10 Probability

Lesson 10.3 Activity: Comparing Experimental and Theoretical Probability

Teacher's Guide

Type of activity	Hands-on activity Foundational activity for students needing extra help
Objectives	Reinforce the skill of finding probability. Compare an experimental probability to a theoretical probability.
Materials	Two fair dice
Time	20–30 min
Ability levels	Mixed
Prerequisite skills	Add two whole numbers. Find the probability of a compound event, given the sample space.
Grouping	Students should work in pairs.
Assessment of students' learning	See Lesson 10.3 Activity: Rubric.

Lesson 10.3 Activity
Rubric

Category	4	3	2	1
Mathematical concepts	Explanation shows complete understanding of the mathematical concepts used to solve the problem(s).	Explanation shows substantial understanding of the mathematical concepts used to solve the problem(s).	Explanation shows some understanding of the mathematical concepts needed to solve the problem(s).	Explanation shows very limited understanding of the underlying concepts needed to solve the problem(s) OR is not written.
Reflection	The reflection shows clear thought and effort. The learning experience being reflected upon is relevant and meaningful to student and learning goals.	The reflection shows a lot of thought and effort. Student makes attempts to demonstrate relevance, but the relevance is unclear in reference to learning goals.	The reflection shows some thought and effort. Some sections of the reflection are irrelevant to student and/or learning goals.	The reflection is superficial. Most of the reflection is irrelevant to student and/or learning goals.

Lesson 10.3 Activity
Comparing Experimental and Theoretical Probability

Step 1   Roll two fair dice. Note the number of dots on the top face of each die. Add the two numbers and record the sum in a tally chart. For example:

Die 1 $\rightarrow$ 2   Die 2 $\rightarrow$ 5   Sum = 2 + 5 = 7

Step 2   Repeat this 36 times. Record your results in the table on the Student Recording Sheet. What do you notice?

Step 3   The table below shows all the possible outcomes when tossing two dice. Use it to find the theoretical probabilities for the sums. Complete the table on the Student Recording Sheet.

Possible Sums for Two Dice

Die 1 + Die 2 ↓ →	1	2	3	4	5	6
1	2	3	4	5	6	7
2	3	4	5	6	7	8
3	4	5	6	7	8	9
4	5	6	7	8	9	10
5	6	7	8	9	10	11
6	7	8	9	10	11	12

Step 4   As you work, think about these questions:

- What are all the possible sums?
- How many possible sums are there?
- What is the least possible sum? Why?
- What is the greatest possible sum? Why?
- What is the most likely sum? Why?

Step 5   Answer the questions on the Student Recording Sheet.

Name: _____   Date: _____

Lesson 10.3 Activity
Student Recording Sheet

Sum	2	3	4	5	6	7	8	9	10	11	12
Observed frequency											
Experimental probability	$\frac{\Box}{36}$	$\frac{\Box}{36}$	$\frac{\Box}{36}$	$\frac{\Box}{36}$	$\frac{\Box}{36}$	$\frac{\Box}{36}$	$\frac{\Box}{36}$	$\frac{\Box}{36}$	$\frac{\Box}{36}$	$\frac{\Box}{36}$	$\frac{\Box}{36}$
Theoretical probability	$\frac{\Box}{36}$	$\frac{\Box}{36}$	$\frac{\Box}{36}$	$\frac{\Box}{36}$	$\frac{\Box}{36}$	$\frac{\Box}{36}$	$\frac{\Box}{36}$	$\frac{\Box}{36}$	$\frac{\Box}{36}$	$\frac{\Box}{36}$	$\frac{\Box}{36}$

1. How many possible outcomes (sums) are there altogether?

2. Why are some sums more likely to occur than others?

3. Compare the experimental and theoretical probabilities of each sum. What do you observe?

Reflection

4. What have you learned from this activity?

CHAPTER 10 Probability

Project: Probability Modeling

Teacher's Guide

Common Core State Standard	7.SP.7b Develop a probability model (which may not be uniform) by observing frequencies in data generated from a chance process.
Objective	Compare an experimental probability model and a theoretical probability model.
Materials	36 geometry cards on pages 117 to 120
Time	20–30 min
Ability levels	Mixed
Prerequisite skill	Find the probability of simple events.
Grouping	Students should work in groups of three to five.
Assessment of students' learning	See Chapter 10 Project: Rubric.

Chapter 10 Project
Rubric

Category	4	3	2	1
Mathematical concepts	Explanation shows complete understanding of the mathematical concepts used to solve the problem(s).	Explanation shows substantial understanding of the mathematical concepts used to solve the problem(s).	Explanation shows some understanding of the mathematical concepts needed to solve the problem(s).	Explanation shows very limited understanding of the underlying concepts needed to solve the problem(s) OR is not written.
Mathematical reasoning	Uses complex and refined mathematical reasoning.	Uses effective mathematical reasoning.	Shows some evidence of mathematical reasoning.	Shows little evidence of mathematical reasoning.
Strategy/ Procedures	Uses an efficient and effective strategy to solve the problem(s).	Uses an effective strategy to solve the problem(s).	Uses an effective strategy to solve the problem(s) but does not do it consistently.	Does not use an effective strategy to solve the problem(s).
Explanation	Explanation is detailed and clear.	Explanation is clear.	Explanation is a little difficult to understand, but includes critical components.	Explanation is difficult to understand and is missing several components OR is not included.
Working with others	Student was an engaged partner, listening to suggestions of others and working cooperatively throughout the lesson.	Student was an engaged partner but had trouble listening to others and/or working cooperatively.	Student cooperated with others, but needed prompting to stay on task.	Student did not work effectively with others.

Chapter 10 Project
Probability Modeling

In this project, your group will carry out an experiment involving geometry cards to develop a probability model. Select either Task A or Task B, and carry out the steps given.

Answer the questions in the Student Recording Sheet for your activity. Then summarize your findings, and prepare a simple presentation to share in class.

Task A – Polygon Cards and Circle Cards

Step 1   Shuffle the 36 geometry cards and lay them face down on the table.

Step 2   Select 10 cards at random.

Step 3   Of these 10 cards, note how many Polygon cards and how many Circle cards you have.

Step 4   Find the relative frequencies (or experimental probabilities) of the two types of cards.

Step 5   Record your result in the probability distribution table on the Student Recording Sheet.

Step 6   Return the cards to the deck and reshuffle.

Step 7   Repeat Steps 2 to 6 ten times.

Step 8   Calculate the average experimental probabilities:

$$\frac{\text{Sum of experimental probability values}}{10}$$

Chapter 10 Project continued
Probability Modeling

Task B – Word Cards and Number Cards

Step 1 Shuffle the 36 geometry cards and lay the deck face down on the table.

Step 2 Select 13 cards at random.

Step 3 Of these 13 cards, note how many are Word cards (GEE, IMA, TREE) and how many are Number cards (1, 2, 3, ..., 9).

Step 4 Find the relative frequencies (or experimental probabilities) of the two types of cards.

Step 5 Record your result in the probability distribution table on the Student Recording Sheet.

Step 6 Return the cards to the deck and reshuffle.

Step 7 Repeat Steps 2 to 6 ten times.

Step 8 Calculate the average experimental probabilities:

$$\frac{\text{Sum of experimental probability values}}{10}$$

Name: _____   Date: _____

Chapter 10 Project
Student Recording Sheet

Task A

Round	Polygon cards		Circle cards	
	Observed frequency	Experimental probability	Observed frequency	Experimental probability
1				
2				
3				
4				
5				
6				
7				
8				
9				
10				
Average				

1. What is the theoretical probability of selecting a Polygon card from the 36 cards?

2. What is the theoretical probability of selecting a Circle card from the 36 cards?

3. Compare the theoretical probabilities and the average experimental probabilities you have found. What do you observe about the values?

Chapter 10 Project continued
Student Recording Sheet

Task B

Round	Word cards		Number cards	
	Observed frequency	Experimental probability	Observed frequency	Experimental probability
1				
2				
3				
4				
5				
6				
7				
8				
9				
10				
Average				

1. What is the theoretical probability of selecting a Word card from the 36 cards?

2. What is the theoretical probability of selecting a Number card from the 36 cards?

3. Compare the theoretical probabilities and the average experimental probabilities you have found. What do you observe about the values?

Chapter 10 Project
Materials

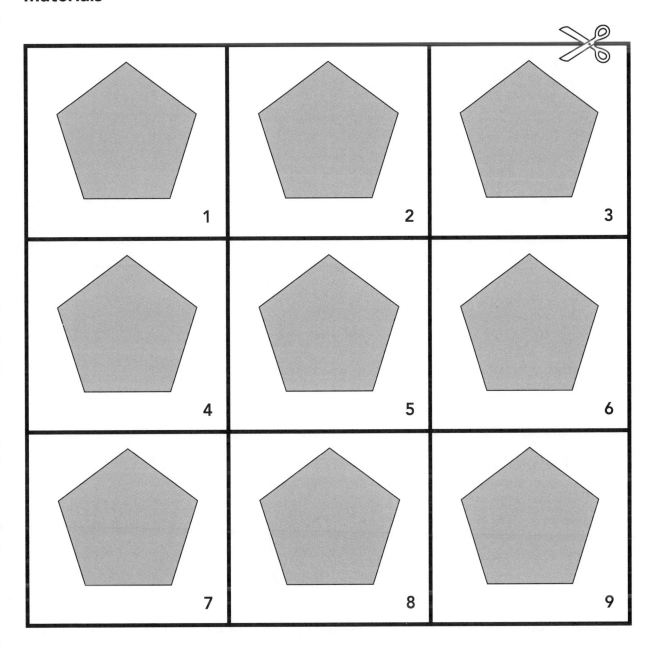

Chapter 10 Project continued
Materials

1

2

3

4

5

6

7

8

9

Chapter 10 Project continued
Materials

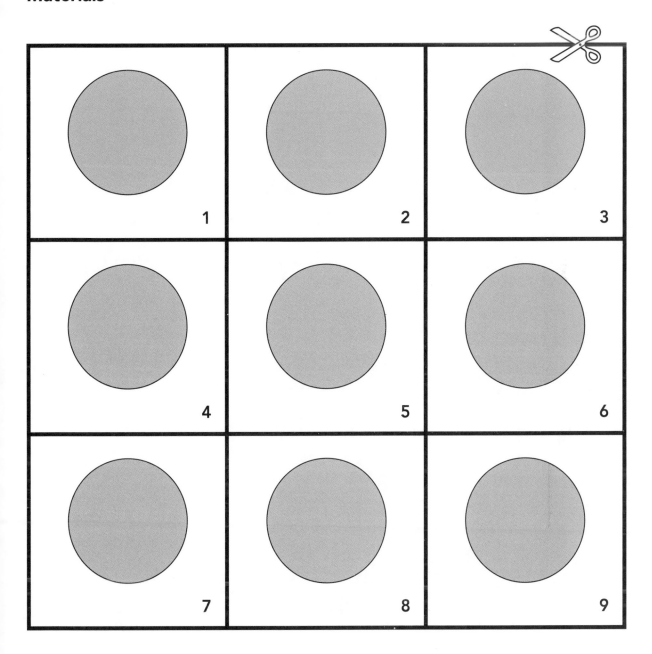

Chapter 10 Project continued
Materials

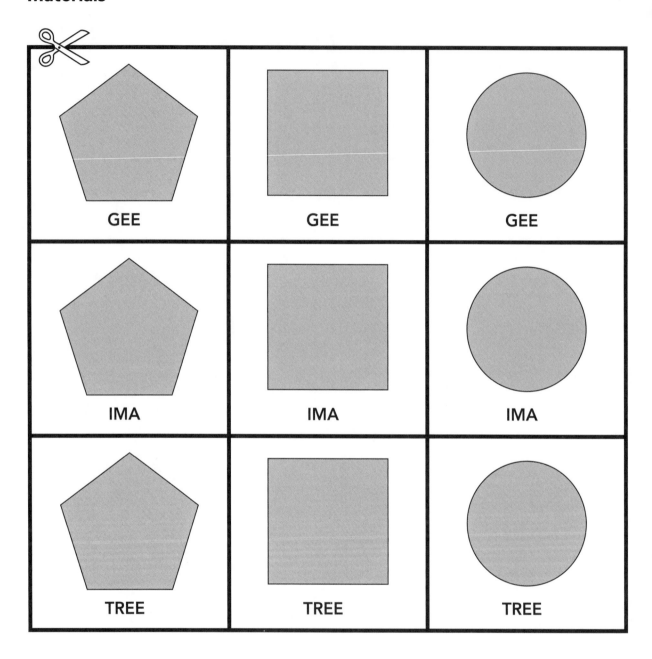

GEE	GEE	GEE
IMA	IMA	IMA
TREE	TREE	TREE

Solutions

Lesson 1.3 Activity (p. 4)

1. Area of the new square formed
   $= 2^2 + 1^2$
   $= 5$ in^2

2. Let s be the length of one side
   of the new square.
   Area of square $= s^2$
   $\qquad\quad 5 = s^2$
   $\qquad\quad s \approx \sqrt{5}$ in.

3. Approximately 2.2 in.

4. a) $\sqrt{5} \approx 2.2$ in.
   b)

5. Answers vary. Sample: Irrational numbers
   cannot be written as terminating or
   repeating decimals. However, they can
   be approximated with rational numbers.

Chapter 1 Project (p. 8)

1. Answers vary, depending on the numbers
   chosen. Students should understand that
   irrational numbers cannot be expressed in
   $\frac{m}{n}$ form, where m and n are integers.

2. Answers vary. Sample: The square root of a
   number is rational if all the prime factors of
   the number have even exponents when it is
   written as the product of its prime factors.

Lesson 2.1 Activity (p. 12)

Answers vary. Sample:

8	3	4
1	5	9
6	7	2

1. The sum of the digits is 45.

2. The sum of the digits used is 3 times the
   sum of one row.

3. Answers vary. Sample:

3	−2	−1
−4	0	4
1	2	−3

4. Yes; 0; 0

Chapter 2 Project (p. 18)

Answers vary. Sample:

Level	Mathematical expression	Answer
1a	−6 + 5	−1
1b	21 − 43	−22
2a	−3 + 42 ÷ 7	3
2b	(9 − 5) × 2	8
2c	8 ÷ (1 + 3)	2
3	5 × 9 − (−6) + (−2)	49

Sample word problem:
On a winter day, the lowest temperature
recorded in a town was −6°C. The highest
temperature recorded was 5°C higher than
the lowest temperature. What was the
highest temperature recorded on that day?

Lessons 3.4 Activity (p. 22)

Answers vary. Sample:

Algebraic expression	Area of rectangle C	Area of rectangle D	Total area of rectangle E
2.1(x + 3)	2.1x	6.3	2.1x + 6.3
0.8(3x + 5)	2.4x	4	2.4x + 4
1.5(2x + 2)	3x	3	3x + 3
3.6(x + 6)	3.6x	21.6	3.6x + 21.6
0.4(5x + 8)	2x	3.2	2x + 3.2

1. Answers vary, but should include the observations that:
   - the area of rectangle C is the product of the decimal and the variable term in the parentheses,
   - the area of rectangle D is the product of the decimal and the constant in the parentheses,
   - the total area of rectangle E is the sum of the areas of rectangle C and rectangle D. It is the expanded form of the algebraic expression.

2. To expand the algebraic expression, we can use the distributive property. The decimal must be multiplied by both terms in the parentheses.

3. Answers vary. Sample: To expand such algebraic expressions, the decimal must be multiplied by each term in the parentheses.

Lessons 3.6 Activity (p. 28)

1. Answers vary. The final answers are the same as the first integer chosen.

2.

Integer	x
Multiply by 2	$x \cdot 2 = 2x$
Subtract 3	$2x - 3$
Divide by 4	$\dfrac{2x - 3}{4}$
Multiply by 12	$\dfrac{2x - 3}{4} \cdot 12 = 3(2x - 3)$ $= 6x - 9$
Add 9	$6x - 9 + 9 = 6x$
Divide by 6	$\dfrac{6x}{6} = x$
Final answer	x

3. Answers vary. Sample: Although four operations are applied to the original number, the operations cancel themselves out.

Chapter 3 Project (p. 32)

1.

Algebraic expression	First term	Second term	Greatest common factor	Factored form
4x + 6y	4x	6y	2	2(2x + 3y)
9x + 3y	9x	3y	3	3(3x + y)
7x + 7y	7x	7y	7	7(x + y)
10x + 15y	10x	15y	5	5(2x + 3y)
4x + 5y	4x	5y	1	4x + 5y
15x + 9y	15x	9y	3	3(5x + 3y)
12x + 8y	12x	8y	4	4(3x + 2y)

2. Answers vary. Sample: The number of groups in the first table and the greatest common factor in the second table are the same. For each algebraic expression, the number of hexagons in each group represents the first term in the parentheses while the number of diamonds in each group represents the second term in the parentheses.

3. Yes, the expression $4x + 5y$ cannot be factored any further. The only common factor is 1.

Lesson 4.1 Activity (p. 38)

The equivalent equations are:
$3x - 7$ and $6x - 7 - 3x$;
$2(y - 7x)$ and $2y - 14x$;
$10x - 5$ and $5x - 5 + 5x$;
$-5x + 2$ and $7 - 5(x + 1)$;
$xy + 12y$ and $y(x + 12)$;
$x(3 - y)$ and $-2xy + 3x + xy$;
$y(-x + 1) + 6$ and $-xy + 6 + y$;
$-6 + 2(y + x)$ and $2(x + y - 3)$;
$\frac{1}{2}(-4y + 1)$ and $-2y + \frac{1}{2}$;
$y - \frac{21}{2}$ and $y - (10 + \frac{1}{2})$;
$\frac{1}{2}(x + y)$ and $\frac{1}{2}x + \frac{1}{2}y$;
$\frac{1}{3}(4x + y) - 1$ and $\frac{4}{3}x + \frac{1}{3}y - 1$.

Lesson 4.2 Activity (p. 44)

1. $\frac{1}{2}x + \frac{1}{3}x + \frac{1}{6}x$
$= \frac{3}{6}x + \frac{2}{6}x + \frac{1}{6}x$
$= \frac{6x}{6}$
$= x$

2. Answers vary. Possible values of x include 6, 12, and 18.

3. The value of x must be a multiple of 6, because it must be divisible by 2 and by 3.

4. $\frac{5}{6}x = 45$; $x = 54$; Mabel bought 54 beads.

5. Answers vary. Sample: $a = 2$, $b = 3$, and $c = 6$.

Chapter 4 Project (p. 48)

1. $50 + x + 25y < 400$

2. Answers vary. The combination chosen should be the most economical and should fall within the budget.

Lesson 5.1 Activity (p. 52)

Answers vary, depending on the order of the rectangles selected.

Number of squares on the vertical side, v	Number of squares on the horizontal side, h	Area of the rectangle, A
5	3	15
5	9	45
5	6	30
5	7	35
5	8	40
5	4	20

1. All of the rectangles have the same width, v.

2. $A = vh$ or $v = \frac{A}{h}$

3. The value of A increases as the value of h increases. A is directly proportional to h.

4. Answers vary. Sample: The two variables A and h are in direct proportion because the ratio $\frac{A}{h}$ is constant for all values of the variables.

Chapter 5 Project (pp. 58–59)

Answers vary depending on the length of the bulletin board and the distance between the stickers. Sample:

Length of bulletin board	120 in.			
Distance between edges of two stickers, x	1	2	3	4
Number of stickers, y	120	60	40	30

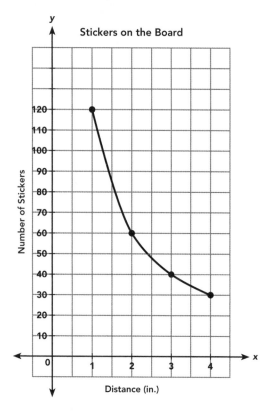

1. Inverse proportion

2. Answers vary. Sample:
   Constant of proportionality = $2 \times 60 = 120$

3. Answers vary. Sample: $xy = 120$

4. Answers vary depending on the data.
   Sample: (2, 60); If the distance between the left edges of two stickers is 2 inches, there will be 60 stickers along the length of the bulletin board.

Lesson 6.1 Activity (p. 64)

Answers vary. Sample:

Complementary angles	$\angle HAK$ and $\angle KAB$ $60° + 30° = 90°$
	$\angle HAK$ and $\angle HKA$ $60° + 30° = 90°$
	$\angle BCK$ and $\angle KCD$ $30° + 60° = 90°$
	$\angle BCK$ and $\angle BKC$ $30° + 60° = 90°$
	$\angle AGC$ and $\angle ACG$ $60° + 30° = 90°$
Supplementary angles	$\angle GKH$ and $\angle HKC$ $30° + 150° = 180°$
	$\angle GKA$ and $\angle AKC$ $60° + 120° = 180°$
	$\angle GFK$ and $\angle KFE$ $90° + 90° = 180°$

Reflection

Answers vary. Sample: When two lines intersect, the sum of the angles on one side of a line is 180°; if one angle of a triangle is a right angle, then the other two angles are complementary angles; two right angles are supplementary angles.

Lessons 6.2–6.3 Activity (p. 70)

1.

Quadrilateral	Number of pairs of congruent angles
Parallelogram	6
Trapezoid	4
Rhombus	6
Rectangle	6

2. The parallelogram, rhombus, and rectangle have the same number of pairs of congruent angles.

3. These quadrilaterals have two pairs of parallel sides.

4. Answers vary. Quadrilaterals with two pairs of parallel sides have four pairs of congruent alternate interior angles. Diagonals in all the quadrilaterals form two pairs of congruent vertical angles.

Chapter 6 Project (p. 74)

Polygon	Number of sides	Sum of interior angles	Sum of exterior angles	Total sum
Triangle	3	180°	360°	540°
Quadrilateral	4	360°	360°	720°
Pentagon	5	540°	360°	900°
Hexagon	6	720°	360°	1,080°

1. 360°

2. 180n°

3. The interior and exterior angles at each vertex are supplementary. The sum of all interior and exterior angles for a polygon with n sides is 180n°. As the sum of exterior angles is 360° regardless of the number of sides, the sum of all interior angles in a polygon with n sides is (180n − 360)°.

Lessons 7.1–7.3 Activity (p. 78)

1. A right triangle

2. 2 in.

3. 5 in.; The radius is half the length of the hypotenuse.

4. No

5. a) Yes
   b) Equilateral triangles have that property.

Chapter 7 Project (p. 82)

1. Answers vary. The opposite angles should be supplementary.

2. Answers vary, but should include the conclusion that the opposite angles of a quadrilateral inscribed in a circle are supplementary.

3. Answers vary. Some examples are a parallelogram that is not a rectangle and a rhombus that is not a square. If the opposite angles of a quadrilateral are not supplementary, a circle will not pass through all the vertices of the quadrilateral.

Lessons 8.2–8.4 Activity (p. 86)

1. 8 in^3

2. Answers vary.

3. Answers vary slightly depending on the measurements.
   Cylinder: 6.28 in^3
   Cone: 2.09 in^3
   Sphere: 4.19 in^3

4. Answers vary.

Chapter 8 Project (p. 94)

1. Answers vary. Find the surface area of the solids using their respective formula and select the shape with the smallest surface area.

2. Jason should choose a cone-shaped paperweight because it has the smallest surface area.

Lesson 9.4 Activity (p. 98)

1. Answers vary, depending on the data collected.

2. Answers vary, depending on the data collected.

3. Answers vary. The mean height of the students in the sample is an approximation of the mean height of the students in the population. However, if there is a great difference between the two mean heights, a possible reason is that the sample contained one or more heights that were much different from the others.

Lesson 9.5 Activity (p. 102)

Answers vary, based on the number of Color A counters in the bag.

Sample: The bag contained 50 white counters and 50 black counters.

Sample	1	2	3	4	5
Number of white counters	4	6	8	4	4

Sample	6	7	8	9	10
Number of white counters	6	5	2	5	4

1. Answers vary.
   Sample:
   $$\frac{4+6+8+4+4+6+5+2+5+4}{10} = 4.8$$

2. Answers vary.
   Sample:
   $$\frac{4.8}{10} = 0.48$$

3. Answers vary.
   Sample:
   $0.48 \times 100 = 48$

4. Answers vary, but the estimated number of Color A counters from question 3 should not differ much from the actual number of Color A counters. Sample: 48 is very close to the actual number of white counters, 50.

5. Answers vary, but should include the observation that the method used in the activity allowed students to make an accurate estimate of the number of colored counters in the bag. Similar methods are used in real life, for example, when estimating the population of a particular species of fish in a pond.

Chapter 9 Project (p. 106)

Answers vary, depending on the extract used. To draw the box plot, students should identify the lower extreme value and the upper extreme value of the data. They should also find the lower quartile, the median, and the upper quartile of the data.

Lesson 10.3 Activity (p. 110)

Observed frequencies and experimental probabilities will vary.

Sum	2	3	4	5	6	7
Theoretical probability	$\frac{1}{36}$	$\frac{2}{36}$	$\frac{3}{36}$	$\frac{4}{36}$	$\frac{5}{36}$	$\frac{6}{36}$

Sum	8	9	10	11	12
Theoretical probability	$\frac{5}{36}$	$\frac{4}{36}$	$\frac{3}{36}$	$\frac{2}{36}$	$\frac{1}{36}$

1. 36

2. The table of all the possible outcomes for the toss of two dice shows that some sums occur more frequently than others because those sums have more number pairs that add up to them. Sample:
   The sum 2 only has (1, 1) as a number pair, while the sum 6 has (1, 5), (2, 4), (3, 3), (4, 2) and (5, 1). This increases the probability of getting the sum 6.

3. The experimental probability is close to, but not equal to, the theoretical probability.

4. Answers vary.

Chapter 10 Project (pp. 115–116)

Task A
Answers vary. Sample:

Round	Polygon cards		Circle cards	
	Observed frequency	Experimental probability	Observed frequency	Experimental probability
1	9	0.9	1	0.1
2	6	0.6	4	0.4
3	7	0.7	3	0.3
4	5	0.5	5	0.5
5	6	0.6	4	0.4
6	8	0.8	2	0.2
7	7	0.7	3	0.3
8	8	0.8	2	0.2
9	7	0.7	3	0.3
10	5	0.5	5	0.5
Average		0.68		0.32

1. $\frac{24}{36} = \frac{2}{3}$, or about 0.67

2. $\frac{12}{36} = \frac{1}{3}$, or about 0.33

3. The average experimental probability of selecting a Polygon card varied only slightly from the theoretical probability, which is $\frac{2}{3}$, or about 0.67. The experimental probability of a Circle card was also very close to its theoretical probability of $\frac{1}{3}$, or about 0.33.

Task B
Answers vary. Sample:

Round	Word cards		Number cards	
	Observed frequency	Experimental probability	Observed frequency	Experimental probability
1	3	$\frac{3}{13}$	10	$\frac{10}{13}$
2	5	$\frac{5}{13}$	8	$\frac{8}{13}$
3	4	$\frac{4}{13}$	9	$\frac{9}{13}$
4	2	$\frac{2}{13}$	11	$\frac{11}{13}$
5	4	$\frac{4}{13}$	9	$\frac{9}{13}$
6	3	$\frac{3}{13}$	10	$\frac{10}{13}$
7	4	$\frac{4}{13}$	9	$\frac{9}{13}$
8	1	$\frac{1}{13}$	12	$\frac{12}{13}$
9	2	$\frac{2}{13}$	11	$\frac{11}{13}$
10	3	$\frac{3}{13}$	10	$\frac{10}{13}$
Average		$\frac{31}{130}$ ≈ 0.24		$\frac{99}{130}$ ≈ 0.76

1. $\frac{9}{36} = \frac{1}{4} = 0.25$

2. $\frac{27}{36} = \frac{3}{4} = 0.75$

3. The average experimental probability of selecting a Word card varied only slightly from the theoretical probability, which is $\frac{1}{4}$, or 0.25. The average experimental probability of selecting a Number card varied only slightly from the theoretical probability, which is $\frac{3}{4}$, or 0.75.

BLANK

BLANK